FLICK and FLAK

MORE POISON CAPSULE REVIEWS

by **E. Basil St. Blaise**

Illustrated by
Randy Jones
&
Martin Kozlowski

Copyright © 2016 Now What Media, LLC
All rights reserved.
No portion of this book may be reproduced
without the express written permission of the publisher.

Front cover by Martin Kozlowski
Illustrations by Randy Jones
(including depictions of Mr. St. Blaise)
& Martin Kozlowski
Edited by Martin Kozlowski

For the latest Critic's Corner reviews,
please visit nowwhatmedia.com

For more on Now What Media Books,
please visit nowwhatmedia.com/nowwhatbooks.html

For more of E. Basil St. Blaise's
Poison Capsule Reviews in print purchase

**Love the Sinner
Hate the Cinema**

available at nowwhatmedia.com

And check out these other
Now What Books

The Golem's Voice

**Further Adventures:
Now What Anthology No. 1**

PK in the Terrarium

Downtown Drowned

The Da Vinci Cold

Go the Fk Back to Work!**

Fairly Grim Tales

Gertrude's Follies

INX Battle Lines

The Illustrators

Randy Jones

Randy Jones was born on a potato farm in Exeter, Ontario, Canada, and he's been drawing pictures since he was a small fry. He was influenced by Koko the Clown cartoons on early television, and by any movie with cowboys and indians, gladiators, pirates, Tarzan, or the Ten Commandments.

His artwork has appeared in many major publications including the *Wall Street Journal*, the *New York Times*, *Playboy*, *Newsday*, and the *National Lampoon*, and in books published by Cambridge University Press, Houghton Mifflin, and Random House.

Randy is a big fan of E. Basil St. Blaise's caustic revues and has been mildly delighted to illustrate them for lo these many years.

Martin Kozlowski

Since 1980 Martin Kozlowski has chronicled the social and political scenes in a wide range of publications including *Barron's*, the *National Law Journal*, the *New York Times*, *Newsday* and the *Wall Street Journal*.

He art directs and contributes to the weekly editorial illustration service *inxart.com*. His comic strips have appeared in a variety of publications including *Fortune* and the *Daily Star* in Beirut, Lebanon. His work has appeared in numerous exhibitions including shows in New York, Paris, Santa Fe, Calgary and Warsaw. He is the editor-in-chief of *nowwhatmedia.com*. He has been asked to dog-sit Josef more than once.

See more of his work at *martinkozlowski.com*.

Greetings from my plush Hollywood East headquarters on wheels (currently, ironically, in Parker, AZ — so maybe Far East.) I'm here along with my faithful mascot, Josef. He's a proud Affenpinscher — a German monkey dog — and he loves bananas and Johnny Weismuller movies (Jungle Jim more than Tarzan, go figure.) And, yes, it's pronounced *Yo*sef, as in von Sternberg.

I'm hard at work on my investigation into celebrity incest entitled *Coming Into Their Own* and Volume II of my acclaimed history of bad costume design, *Fitting Punishment*. As well as *Zipper Locks*, a study of the intimate grooming styles of the stars. Not to mention preparing my course *Pleasant Oaters: Classic Westerns That Don't Reek* for the proposed Andy Devine College Prep in nearby Salome. *Oops*, I just did mention. I hate self-promotion, but if you're looking for a surefire investment, and the idea of commemorative gold coins featuring the faces of famous best boys sounds irresistable, let's talk.

But I've taken time off from my busy La La Land schedule (and part-time gig at Safeway) to host this second collection of the best Poison Capsule Reviews from the Critic's Corner. Let me begin by answering the three questions I'm asked most often:

1) What qualifies you to pass judgment on the hard work of dedicated film professionals?
How does a certificate from Sandy Kenyon's online Movie Blurb Institute <u>and</u> a James MacArthur grant <u>and</u> a tape collection that runs into the hundreds grab ya?

2) What critic or critics or critiques inspired you when you were first starting out?
There were so many, but Ambrose Bierce's 'The covers of this book are too far apart.' struck a nerve.

3) Why don't you like more movies?
When they start making 'em like they used to, I'll start liking 'em like…I like…like they used to.

2012 Oscar race with Octavia Spencer in *The Help*, Meryl Streep in *The Iron Lady* on *War Horse*, George Clooney in *The Descendants*, Jean Dujardin in *The Artist*, & Ben Kingsley in *Hugo*. *The Artist* won Best Picture.

Many of my 2012 notices were included in a previous compendium. This batch embraces the all-important Holiday Season when stressed shoppers sinking into debt are entertained by Prestige Pictures. These tend to feature gender confusion, mental disability, limps, internment, SS uniforms and strained accents. It's the time of year when Studios celebrate by releasing Oscar bait, typically just off the Santa Monica pier where Industry sharks go for their feeding frenzies.

Quelle surprise! The year's Best Picture Oscar winner was a French film, *The Artist*. The filmmakers avoided the subtitle problem (Americans would rather read health warnings on bacon) by making it a silent (note to Godard!) I loathe mimes, but it did feature Uggie, the most adorable *petit chien*. Josef was *sooo* jealous.

The Master
— Of the louse.

Finding Nemo 3D
— Open to deep bait.

Resident Evil: Retribution
— Payback…the patrons.

Arbitrage
— Bare market.

10 Years
— Hard labor.

Lawless
— Prohibition error.

Bachelorette
— Wed dreams.

The Words
— Rough writer.

The Inbetweeners
— Middling.

Girl Model — Pedo files.

Beauty Is Embarrassing — Then this is a beauty.

The Eye of the Storm — Becalmed.

Joaquin Phoenix must serve *The Master*. But which one? Philip Seymour Hoffman or L. Ron Hubbard?

Evildoers meet their match in *Judge Dredd 3D*.

Dredd 3D — *Dredd* lox.
Perks of Being a Wallflower — Shyer education.
Trouble With the Curve — Every Which Way But Lucid.
House at the End of the Street — Dead end skids.
About Cherry — The pits.
End of Watch — Patrol bloat.
How to Survive a Plague — Antidotal evidence.
Diana Vreeland…
The Eye Has to Travel — Harpy's bizarre.
Wuthering Heights — Moors the pity.
Hotel Transylvania — The service sucks.
Looper — L'*oops!*
Won't Back Down — A taught drama.
Solomon Kane — *Solomon* grungy.

....

Pitch Perfect — Tone deaf.
Taken 2 — The cleaners.
Sinister — Lefty frazzle.
V/H/S — Pause.
Just 45 Minutes From Broadway — In a dumpster down an alley.
The Paperboy — Doesn't deliver.
Butter — Balls!
Not Fade Away — Why not?
Seven Psychopaths — Crazy shit.
Argo — Naught.
Here Comes the Boom — Badder *Boom*.
3,2,1…Frankie Go Boom — And bust.

Smashed — Beasts of bourbon.
Atlas Shrugged: Part 2 — Rand pall.
Alex Cross — A heavy Cross to bear.
Paranormal Activity 4 — The new *Paranormal*.
Holy Motors — Combustion my chops.
The Sessions — Lame ass.
Nobody Walks — Everybody runs…from this.
Codebreaker — Turing company.
Frankenweenie — Dawg of the dead.

Frankenweenie discharges on his nightly walk.

Daniel Craig's James Bond awaits HRH in *Skyfall*.

Skyfall
— Craig lists.
The First Time
— Virgin on the ridiculous.
Cloud Atlas
— They can't be cirrus.
Chasing Mavericks
— Surf n' turd.
Silent Hill: Revelation 3D
— *Hill*-conceived.
Fun Size
— Not too big to fail.
The Loneliest Planet — Sphere and loathing.
Pusher
— Junk feud.
Sleep Tight
— Go to bed drunk.
Wreck-It Ralph — Wrecked-'em.

Flight — Dick.
The Bay — Of pigs.
This Must Be the Place — Penn & smeller.
The Last Quartet — Be four-warned.
The Details — Spare me.
A Liar's Autobiography — Glam Chapman.
The Man With the Iron Fists — On which the director sits.
The Twilight Saga: Breaking Dawn Part 2 — Twi *fie*.
Anna Karenina — A train wreck.
Silver Linings Playbook — Manic Cooper.
Rust and Bone — Corrode-pleaser.
Hitler's Children — Mother Goose steppers.
Barrymore — The Not-So-Great Profile.
Hitchcock — *Psycho* babble.
Life of Pi — Lemon *Pi*.

Red Dawn — Pretty *Dawn* funny.
Rise of the Guardians — Guardian-variety.
The Central Park Five — Rape nut serial.
The Collection — Of Hummels.
Universal Soldier: Day of Reckoning — *Universal* plug-ugly.
Dragon — Ballz.
Silent Night — Holey Night.
Hecho En Mexico — Mextapes.
Hyde Park on Hudson — Hyde and go suck.
Beware of Mr. Baker — Ginger snaps.
....

Playing for Keeps — And creeps.
Lay the Favorite — For bettor or worse.
Deadfall — A ton of pricks.
Tchoupitoulas — The Big Queasy.
Love, Marilyn — Not particularly.
The Normals — Stock options.
Bad Kids Go to Hell — And watch this.
The Rabbi's Cat — Katz n' jabber.
The Fitzgerald Family Christmas — Creche test dummies.
Killing Them Softly — With his schlong.

Hitman Brad Pitt tries to get his weapon up to hit a hard target in *Killing Them Softly*.

Gandalf commands Bilbo & friends to build toys from *The Hobbit: An Unexpected Journey*.

The Hobbit: An Unexpected Journey — Filthy Hobbits.

Any Day Now — Too soon.

Save the Date — Save the money.

Yelling to the Sky — A howler.

This is 40 — Miles of bad road.
Zero Dark Thirty — Bin Laden-di-da.
Monsters, Inc. 3D — Workers' frights.
The Guilt Trip — Mother load.
Jack Reacher — Reacher 'round.
Amour — Or less.
The Impossible — Tsunami on rye.
On the Road — Kerouac jobs.
Cirque Du Soleil: Worlds Away 3D — Tumble bums.
Les Misérables — Lame is.
Parental Guidance — Cramp parents.
Promised Land — Frickin' frack.
Quartet — On all fours.
Barbara — *Oy* Doktor.
Django Unchained — Unchained malady.

Django (Jamie Foxx), aided by Dr. King Schultz (Christoph Waltz), aims to rescue his wife Broomhilda from slavery in *Django Unchained*.

Oscar's 2013 box contained Quvenzhané Wallis in *Beasts of the Southern Wild*, Jennifer Lawrence in *The Silver Linings Playbook*, Jamie Foxx in *Django Unchained*, Richard Parker in *The Life of Pi*, Daniel Day-Lewis in *Lincoln*, & Ben Affleck in *Argo*. *Life of Pi* won Best Picture.

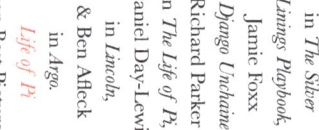

The night before the Oscars, Hollywood gazillionaires get to pretend they're just hipsters with benefits as they rub shoulders with the great unwatched who are feted at The Independent Spirit Awards. Indie film is sorta the minors for the Studios' Big Show — the Silver Lake Mumblecores to the LA Tax Dodgers.

And the host is always some smug kinda-comic like this year's Andy Samberg, the 'alt' Adam Sandler. The bronzed participants bend over backwards pretending they're above trawling for trophies then nearly sprain their arms patting themselves on the back. It's like Tantrick Yoga.

And 2013's underdog winner? Smash semi-sitcom *The Silver Linings Playbook*. This one cured my indie jones.

Texas Chainsaw 3D — Leatherfarce.

A Dark Truth — Not dark enough — I could see it.

56 Up — Middle age spreads.

Crawlspace — Crawling *to* the wreckage.

Gangster Squad — Gangnumb style.

Sean Penn & Ryan Gosling play Cops 'n' Robbers in *Gangster Squad*.

Schwarzenneger & his ex in revenge drama *The Last Stand*.

Parker — Pussy.
John Dies at the End — Of embarrassment.
Yossi — *Chaim*osexuals.
Bullet to the Head — In one ear, out the other.
Stand Up Guys — No, sit down.

The Last Stand
— Snooze *Stand*.
Broken City
— Urban dick, *eh?*
Mama — Crass idiot.
Haunted House
— Shit-level.
Storage 24 — Cache poor.
Struck By Lightning
— Nuts and bolts.
$ellebrity — Pooperazzi.
The Baytown Outlaws
— Killer delete.
Movie 43 — Boor wars.

Zombie hunk Nicholas Hoult hooks up with Kate Moss for a light snack in *Warm Bodies*.

Warm Bodies
— Blown off corpse.
Saving Lincoln
— Start with the one in your pocket.
The Gatekeepers
— Shin Bet noir.
Sound City
— Tracks star.
Resolution — 0 dpi.
Knife Fight — Slitheads.
Koch — DeadEd.
Identity Thief
— ID flies.
Side Effects
— Mostly nausea.
Caesar Must Die
— *Ehh*, too.
Lore — Criminal *Lore*.

Gemma Arterton & Jeremy Renner eye their prey in *Hansel & Gretel: Witch Hunters*.

Hansel and Gretel: Witch Hunters — Witchcrapt.

The Sorcerer and the White Snake — You'd think he could take a hair band.

A Glimpse Inside the Mind of Charles Swan III — A glance half empty.

Top Gun: An IMAX 3D Experience — Jet lag.

A Good Day To Die Hard — Bruise *Willis*.

Beautiful Creatures — Broad casters.

Safe Haven — Shelter skelter.

Escape From Planet Earth 3D — Space lam.

No — Way.

Like Someone in Love — With triviality.

The Haunting in Connecticut 2: Ghosts of Georgia — *Georgia* dreck.

The Power of Few — *Pheww!*

Dwayne Johnson dishes the dirt in *Snitch*.

Snitch — Stoolie noted.

Dark Skies — U Eff Hole.

Bless Me, Ultima — Nothing to sneeze at.

Inescapable — I didn't get off.

11 Flowers — Petal to the meddle.

Rubberneck — Because it's a car wreck.

The Package — Is empty.

Future Weather — A topical depression.

21 and Over — Buzzedcocks.

The Last Exorcism Part II — The devil take it up the hindmost.

Phantom — Menace.

Stoker — Uncle creepy.

The End of Love — A jeerjerker.

A Place at the Table — The hunger games.
Leviathan — Mopy dick.
Hava Nagila: The Movie — A hora film.
Dead Man Down — Bury gaudy.
The ABCs of Death — That's all, she rote.
Emperor — Hiro*heehee*to.
The Monk — Oh, brother!
Somebody Up There Likes Me — Somebody up there is lying.
Don't Stop Believin': Everyman's Journey — Just stop singin'.
Jack the Giant Slayer — Beans dork.

General Fallon can't figure out where his human enemy is hiding in *Jack the Giant Slayer*.

The Incredible Burt Wonderstone — Slight. Off-hand.
The Call — Put on hold.
Spring Breakers — New bile.
Upside Down — Topsy turkey.
Welcome to the Punch — Drunk.
My Amityville Horror — *My Own Private Horrorshow*.
Old Goats — Just goats to show you.
The Kitchen — Table.

....

Olympus Has Fallen — And can't get up.
Admission — Not worth the price of.
InAPPropriate Comedy — UnAPPealing.
The Sapphires — Aboriginal sin.
Love and Honor — GI bull.
Starbuck — Sperm wail.
My Brother the Devil — Hell boy.
Finding Joy — My comical romance.
Le Pont du Nord — *Le Pont* of no return.
Oz the Great and Powerful — Baum to fail.

James Franco & Michelle Williams perform for the director who has almost everything in *Oz the Great and Powerful*.

The prehistoric family rudely salutes their animated forbears in *The Croods*.

The Croods — Caves.

The Host — Meyers lemon.

G.I. Joe: Retaliation — *Joe* sics pack.

Temptation — To guffaw.

The Place Beyond the Pines — *Pines*-sized.

Room 237 — Third degree redrum.

Blancanieves — Snow *What?*

Wrong — Right.

....

The Company You Keep — Flee radicals.

Evil Dead — Gore exercises.

Mental — Psych wart.

Renoir — Two of a père

Trance — Incidental.

Jurassic Park: An IMAX 3D Experience — Tyranno-sore-ass Rex.

Upstream Color — Yellow.

The Brass Teapot — Whistle blower.

Tom Cruise sends out the clones in *Oblivion*.

Benedict Cumberbatch's true identity simply shocks Chris Pine & Zachary Quinto in *Star Trek Into Darkness*.

Oblivion — Rush limbo.
Lotus Eaters — Pleasure crews.
Andre Gregory: Before and After Dinner — Gregory peckish.
Stevie Nicks: In Your Dreams — Stevie nix.
42 — Blackball.
Scary Movie V — Horror *duh* har har.
To the Wonder — Windy Malick.
Disconnect — Plug and pray.
The Angels' Share — A loft.
Antiviral — Bring Purell.

....

Star Trek Into Darkness — Khan game.
Paris-Manhattan — Woody ailin'.
The Lords of Salem — Salem's slop.
In the House — Maison, dicks in.
The Big Wedding — Union buster.
Mud — In your eye.
Kon Tiki — Rift raft.
The Reluctant Fundamentalist — Radical I slam.
At Any Price — I wouldn't see it.
The Numbers Station — Down for the count.
Midnight's Children — Rushdie hour.

Love Is All You Need — How about a decent script?

Arthur Newman — Love at Firth sight.

Home Run — Baseless.

Paradise: Lost — So's the director.

Iron Man 3 — Ferrous dueller.

The Ice Man — Bummeth.

What Maisie Knew — A *Maisie* divorce.

Kiss of the Damned — Vampire weakened.

You Will Be My Son — Foul heir.

Scatter My Ashes at Bergdorf's — You can't keep a Goodman down.

Pain & Gain — Hammy roids.

Anthony Mackie, Dwayne Johnson & Mark Wahlberg work over a kidnapped Tony Shahloub in *Pain & Gain*.

John Goodman sucks down Bradley Cooper, Zach Galifianakis, Ed Helms & Ken Jeong in *The Hangover Part II*.

The Hangover Part III — Wolfpack it in.
Peeples — Wee, the *Peeples*.
Aftershock — Tremortized.
Sightseers — Tour de farce.
Stories We Tell — Polleyannaish.
The Painting — Sketchy.
Venus and Serena — Ace relations.
Frances Ha — Laughable.

Fast & Furious 6 — Skidder-ma-rinky-dink.
Epic – Fail.
Before Midnight — Late-night slack.
The Great Gatsby — Effed Scott Fitzgerald.
The English Teacher — Death sentences.
Black Rock — Blah crock.
We Steal Secrets: The Story of Wikileaks — Leak soup.
Fill the Void — With caulk.

After Earth — Like father, don't like son.

Now You See Me — *Depressed-o change-o!*

The Kings of Summer — Sweat pans.

The East — *East* meets waste.

Shadow Dancer — Froth IRA.

The Purge — Emetic aid.

Much Ado About Nothing — Nothing doo dooing.

Wish You Were Here — To share the pain.

Violet & Daisy — Teeny boppers.

....

This Is The End — You suck on.

The Bling Ring — Don't *Bling* me down.

Between Us — Twixt and shout.

Vehicle 19 — Rental breakdown.

Pandora's Promise — Dick in a box.

Berberian Sound Studio — Post-sinking.

More Than Honey — Oh, *bee-hive!*

Hatchet III — Bury it.

The Internship — Google gloss.

Vince Vaughn & Owen Wilson suck up to the big boss in *The Internship*.

The Guillotines — Necks to nothing.

The Stroller Strategy — Pram tough.

Far Out Isn't Far Enough: The Tomi Ungerer Story — Tomi toons.

World War Z — More dead than alive.

Maniac — Not crazy about it.

A Hijacking — From shit to shore.

Unfinished Song — Hum job.

....

The Attack — I remember bomber.

Time Zero: The Last Year of Polaroid Film — Underdeveloped.

Compulsion — Do in what comes naturally.

The Heat — Fuzz busters.

White House Down — I'm depressed now, too.

I'm So Excited! — Spanish fly.

Redemption — Redeem-witted.

Byzantium — Tired blood.

Man of Steel — *Steel* wooly.

A Band Called Death — *Death* blows.

Detention of the Dead — After ghoul special.

The Lone Ranger — Heave-ho Silver!

Despicable Me 2 — *D'oh* minions.

The Way, Way Back — *Aiee! Way Way.*

The Look of Love — Smut and chaff.

Stuck in Love — Pulpy *Love*.

Kevin Hart: Let Me Explain — I'm just not funny.

Hammer of the Gods — Absence of mallets.

Man of Steel Henry Cavill uses his x-ray vision on Amy Adams' Lois Lane to find his missing undies.

Sulley & Randy improvise a beer bong for Mike in *Monsters University*.

Monsters University — Beast in class.
Just Like a Woman — With two boobs.
Absence — Makes the hard grow fonder.
Pacific Rim — Job.
Killing Season — Dead fall.
Fruitvale Station — Black BART.
V/H/S/2 — Eject.
The Hunt — Hell 'n' *Hunt*.
Still Mine — Never *Mine*.
Crystal Fairy — *Crystal* mess.

Million dollar babies Spade, James, Sandler & Rock in *Grown Ups 2*.

The Wolverine goes native in Japan.

Grown Ups 2 — Infantile paralysis.
R.I.P.D. — Over my dead bobby.
Red 2 — Same old same old.
Turbo — Snail biting.
Dealin' With Idiots — Behind the camera.
The Conjuring — Wraith baiting.
Only God Forgives — But not this.
Girl Most Likely — To suck seed.
Blackfish — Scales down.
The Act of Killing — Brain cells.
Broken — Promise.
The To Do List — Laid paper.
Frankenstein's Army — Military corpse.

....

The Wolverine — Icky and scratchy.
The Servant — Harrumphy Bogarde.
Born in Chicago — Chi of a full deck.
2 Guns — Mug shots.
The Smurfs 2 — The blue nil.
The Canyons — Canyon raunch.
Top Cat: The Movie — Mewl train.
The Spectacular Now — *Now* and thin.
Europa Report — Continental drift.
When Comedy Went to School — And flunked out.
Elysium — Down on their luxe.
Planes — Wing ding-a-ling.

Percy Jackson: Sea of Monsters — *Jackson* hole.

The Happy Poet — Bard vibes.

Linda Lovelace — Esophagus now.

Prince Avalanche — Shit rolls downhill.

In a World… — Of hurt.

I Give It a Year — I give it a week.

Kick-Ass 2 — Mask confusion.

Jobs — Steve maddened.

Ain't Them Bodies Saints — Really, really *Badlands*.

Austenland — Pain Jane.

You Will Be My Son — Pater rabid.

Paranoia — No, I truly am out to get this.

Cutie and the Boxer — Punch and doody.

The World's End — The hurt lager.

We're the Millers — Grass blowers.

Stash test dummies Jennifer Aniston, Will Poulter, Emma Roberts and Jason Sudeikis in *We're the Millers*.

Oprah employs her own help readying for her closeup with Forest Whitaker in *Lee Daniels' The Butler.*

Lee Daniels' The Butler — Uncanny valet.

You're Next — Queue tips.

The Mortal Instruments: City of Bones — Humerus.

The Frozen Ground — Whore frost.

Drinking Buddies — Punks drunk.

One Direction: This Is Us — Us and dim.

The Lifeguard — Drown syndrome.

The Grandmaster — Flash.

The Trials of Muhammad Ali — Feat of Clay.

Passion — Pit.

Empire State — *Empire* of the scum.

The Family — Mob and Dad.

Michelle Pfeiffer & Robert De Niro work over their ancestors in *The Family.*

Vin Diesel takes his seeing-eye alien-dingo-beast for a walk in *Riddick*.

Riddick — Ulous.
Getaway — From me.
Closed Circuit — Short, too.
Salinger — JDate.
Adore — Jam.
Hell Baby — Hater tot.
Winnie Mandela — Winnie: the poop.
Red Obsession — Bordeaux patrol.
Touchy Feely — Massageynistic.
A Teacher — Lesson the load.
Insidious: Chapter 2 — Scarce stiff.

Wadjda — Expect?
Jayne Mansfield's Car — Check out those air bags.
And While We Were Here — There is no there *Here*.
Plush — And minus.
GMO OMG — Food in mouth disease.
Harry Dean Stanton: Partly Fiction — Harry potty.
Money for Nothing: Inside the Federal Reserve — Right said Fed.

....

Prisoners — Detainee boppers.
Thanks for Sharing — TMI.
Enough Said — His and hush.
The Face of Love — Mug whomp.
Generation Iron — Tales from the ripped.
Ip Man: The Final Fight — *Ip* displacement.
The Colony — Frost nixin'.
I Spit on Your Grave 2 — Well, loogie here!

Rush — Rats race.
Jewtopia — A tribe called kvetch.
Cloudy with a Chance of Meatballs 2 — Food fright.
Don Jon — A jerk off.
Gravity — A drag.

Sandra Bullock & George Clooney hang on for dear life in *Gravity*.

Captain Phillips
— Hot Somalis.

Baggage Claim
— Rotator guff.

Metallica Through the Never
— Metal midgets.

We Are What We Are
— Which is boring.

As I Lay Dying
— Put a Faulkner in it.

Runner Runner
— Bummer bummer.

A.C.O.D. — Piece.

Argento's Dracula 3D — Depth valley.

Bad Milo! — Butt gusting.

All the Boys Love Mandy Lane — Puny *Lane*.

Romeo and Juliet — Mount-a-goose and Crapulet.

Tom Hanks' Captain Phillips & his First Mate are menaced by Muse, Barkhad Abdi's Somali pirate.

....

American Hustle
— Flabscam.

The Dirties
— Wooly bully.

Grace Unplugged
— Juiceless.

Machete Kills
— Hack work.

CBGB
  Punko squad.

Broadway Idiot
— Green *Doy*.

A Love That Hurts
— Anal.

Carrie
— Gash and Carrie.

Escape Plan
— Bull pen.

Rosalyn (Jennifer Lawrence), Irving (Christian Bale), Sydney (Amy Adams) & Sheik Yerbouti do the *American Hustle*.

12 Years a Slave — Low yield bonds.
All Is Lost — Seas and desist.
Kill Your Darlings — Beats to a pulp.
The Fifth Estate — WackiLeaks.
Big Ass Spider! — Hasn't got legs.
The Counselor — At loss.
Jackass Presents: Bad Grandpa — Gramps cracker.

....

Blue Is the Warmest Color — Lez is more.
I Am Divine — Punk flamingos.
Last Vegas — Lost *Vegas*.
Ender's Game — Dead *Ender's*.
Free Birds — Turkey club.
Dallas Buyers Club — AIDS and abets.
Thor: The Dark World — Ass god.
Inside Llewyn Davis — Simple folk.

Oscar Isaac of *Inside Llewyn Davis* faces off with a real folk legend.

Donald Sutherland wants JLaw to hotfoot it in *The Hunger Games: Catching Fire*.

The Hunger Games: Catching Fire — Chick lit.

Diana — Princess of wails.

The Book Thief — Tome it may concern.

Last Love — Final score.

Underdogs — You find this.

Great Expectations — Pip squeak.

Elsa tries to warm up Olaf in *Frozen*.

Frozen — Stiff.
Best Man Down — Aisle be damned.
The Armstrong Lie — Lance boils.
The Starving Games — Dundernourished.
The Wind Rises — In Miyazaki's shorts.
At Berkeley — School of rot.
Birth of the Living Dead — Cheesier Romero.
Nebraska — Dern tootin'.
The Best Man Holiday — May the best man wince.
Charlie Countryman — LaBeouf stews.
Dear Mr. Watterson — Calvin and hobbled.

The Great Beauty — Pretty? *Puh-lease!*
Delivery Man — Seed the error of his ways.
Philomena — Misplaced youth.
The Christmas Candle — Snuff film.
Narco Cultura — El dope-a.
Bettie Page Reveals All — Wimps and chains.
Oldboy — Bad *Oldboy*.
Mandela: Long Walk to Freedom — Plodding.
The End of Time — Hour town.
Homefront — Take home pain.
Walking With Dinosaurs — Staggersaurus.
Out of the Furnace — The first one who smelt it…
Night Train to Lisbon — Smooth as the eponymous wine.

The Hobbit: The Desolation of Smaug — *Smaug* alert.
Saving Mr. Banks — HellzaPoppins.
Tyler's Perry's A Madea Christmas — A muddier Christmas.
Anchorman 2: The Legend Continues — *Anchor* management.
The Unknown Known — Ginned Rummy.
Her — To Siri With Love.
Black Nativity — Homey for the holidays.
47 Ronin — *Ronin* martyr's laugh-in.
The Secret Life of Walter Mitty — *Mitty* life crisis.
JFK: A President Betrayed — Pedestrian crossing.
The Invisible Woman — What the Dickens?!
Grudge Match — Punch and jowly.
August: Osage County — *Osage*, can you see?
Lone Survivor — Ambush league.
Justin Bieber's Believe — Bieb, Bieb, yer ass.
The Wolf of Wall Street — Howl to succeed in business.

Jordan Belfort (Leonardo DiCaprio) and Donnie Azoff (Jonah Hill) feel extremely bullish in *The Wolf of Wall Street*.

Classic Critic's Corner

Vintage Joker, Batman & Superman square off against the rebooted Dark Knight, Man of Steel & Bane.

Meh & Superman

The comic book movie genre has featured more reboots than a 60s-themed drag dance-a-thon. Every few years popular characters apparently need to be reimagined for a new generation — if one defines a generation as lasting five years. And with each do-over the vision grows darker and drearier — the heroes more somber than super. As Batman morphed from West to Clooney to Bale, DC swooped from PC to AC/DC to BDSM. *Ugh*.

Villains no longer have relatable goals, like wanting to steal priceless jewels or make the entire human race bow to their will. Instead they're bin Ladens on bath salts or genetically-altered Jeffrey Dahmers. And the identity crises of the so-called good guys are so deep that these schizy souls can barely utter their own supernames. Under the aegis of Christopher Nolan, Bruce Wayne is now semi-batshit crazy and Krypton's lovable lunk has been resurrected as a violence-prone Jesus wannabe with abs of steel. To quote Nolan's own Joker, "Why so serious?"

Let me fix my detractor beam on the genre as it evolved from simpler origins. The days of innocence. Of our youth. Brightly-colored pajama costumes. Table cloth capes. Cardboard swords. Beating the crap out of siblings. Watch out! I've set the Review-O-Ray to *Liquefy!*

Superman and the Mole Men (1951) — A dermatologist removes them.

Batman (1966) — Pow! Bam! *Flop!*

Superman (1978) — The Donner party.

Superman II (1980) — Reeve gauche.

Swamp Thing (1982) — Fen fen.

Superman III (1983) — Pryor offense.

Supergirl (1984) — Flight risk.

Howard the Duck (1986) — No harm, no fowl.

Superman IV: The Quest for Peace (1987) — Cape clod.

The Return of Swamp Thing (1989) — Bloody, miry.

Batman (1989) — Dick Burton.

The Punisher (1989) — Painful.

Captain America (1990) — Cap and trite.

Batman Returns (1992) — My stomach.

The Fantastic Four (1994) — What a revoltin' development.

Batman Forever (1995) — Foul Kilmer.

Batman and Robin (1997) — Nipple slip.

Blade (1998) — All-day sucker.

X-Men (2000) — Douche x machina.

Blade II (2002) — Plasma sweet.

Spider-Man (2002) — Stan Lee tools.

Daredevil (2003) — Unsight training.

X2: X-Men United (2003) — Magneato!

Hulk (2003) — Gammapus.

Hellboy (2004) — Horn dog.

The Punisher (2004) — Recap in yo ass.

Spider-Man 2 (2004) — Doc ach!

Catwoman (2004) — Hollow kitty.

Blade: Trinity (2004) — Fang gorier.

The questers after Oscar 2014: Sandra Bullock in *Her*, Chiwetel Ejiofor in *Gravity*, Amy Adams in *12 Years a Slave*, Leonardo DiCaprio in *American Hustle*, Jared Leto in *The Wolf of Wall Street*, Judy Dench in *The Dallas Buyers Club*, *Frozen* & *Despicable Me 2*. *12 Years a Slave* won Best Picture.

2014

By 2014 all the movie fan site message boards were abuzz with references to the 'MCU'. I thought it might be the school where Georgie Jessel learned to host Friars Club Roasts. Rasheed, the aspiring rapper parked across the way, assumed it was the college where Tupac was tutored in rap.

Turns out it's the Marvel Cinematic Universe, an interlinked system of Superhero pictures. The producers hope moviegoers are as uncritically completist as comics collectors. To me these films are like the *Fast and Furious* franchise: You screen one, you screen 'em all.

Labor Day — Laborious.

Paranormal Activity: The Marked Ones — They all got D-.

Open Grave — In which to lower this.

The Legend of Hercules — Herc, he jerky.

Hercules (Kellan Lutz) gives his fan boys a charge in *The Legend of Hercules*.

Chris Pine in *Jack Ryan: Shadow Recruit* confronts 21st-century, state-of-the-art Russian spycraft.

That Awkward Moment — Stretched to 94 minutes.
12 O'Clock Boys — Noon committal.
Knights of Badassdom — Bad as dumb.

A client of Rob Lowe's Dr. Jack Startz wants to look just like Aaron Eckhart in *I, Frankenstein*.

Jack Ryan: Shadow Recruit — *Ryan*, seek rest.
Interior. Leather Bar. — Gaydar aid.
The Rocket — Fizzles.
The Truth About Emanuel — *Emanuel*: axe.
Cold Comes the Night — Try Nyquil.
Return to Nuke 'Em High — Tromatic.
Ride Along — Drive by.
The Nut Job — Acorn dog.

I, Frankenstein — I for Idiot.
Gimme Shelter — Gimme a break.
Gloria — Is stiff 'un.
Enemies Closer — But no cigar.
Run & Jump — In the lake.
At Middleton — Muddled on.
Best Night Ever — For masochists.
Brightest Star — Twinkle toast.
Reasonable Doubt — Ever dense.
Life of a King — Chess thumping.

Devil's Due — Doo.
Old Goats — Ram rot.
Generation War — Anschlusshy.
Tim's Vermeer — Oil change.
Hank — Pat Paulson.
The Lego Movie — Leggo.
Vampire Academy — Dental school.
A Fantastic Fear of Everything — Scared straight to video.
After the Dark — Doof nukem.
Cavemen — Cro magnum opus.
A Field in England — *Field* and scream.
Welcome to the Jungle — Tropic blunder.
Nurse 3-D — Neofatal.
The Monuments Men — Muster of fine arts.

Frank Stokes (George Clooney) & James Granger (Matt Damon) rescue invaluable treasures of Western Culture in *The Monuments Men*.

Someone Marry Barry — Hubba-hubby.

The Pretty One — *Pretty* poison.

Kids for Cash — Small change.

Winter's Tale — Frost entry.

About Last Night — Shtup making sense.

Endless Love — Ernest & young.

Adult World — Erratica.

The Returned — Because it was defective.

Jimmy P. — *P.* doody.

The New Black — Best bi.

Girl On a Bicycle — Cycle sister.

Date and Switch — Virgin immobile.

3 Days to Kill — 102 minutes to kill.

RoboCop — Tech's mechs.

Robocop nails a mechanized perp on morals charges.

Milo (Kit Harrington) fails to suppress an eruption in *Pompeii*.

Pompeii — Lava boy.

In Secret — Raquin ruin.

Black Out — Senseless violence.

Omar — Little.

Barefoot — Corny.

Liam Neeson tracks down an air-borne menace in *Non-Stop*.

Non-Stop — Plane and simple.

Child's Pose — Pouter outage.

Elaine Stritch… Shoot Me — Full of demerol.

Son of God — *God* awful.

Stalingrad — Siege heil.

The Bag Man — *Bag* of boners.

Anchorman 2: Super-sized R-rated Version — Ranker man.

Odd Thomas — *Thomas* dull be.

Repentance — Unforgivable.

....

The Lunchbox — Pack it in.

Chlorine — Dirty pool.

The Grand Budapest Hotel — Lobby cards.

Mr. Peabody & Sherman — Needs fixing.

In Fear — Terrorble.

Grand Piano — Trill kill.

Jodorowsky's Dune — Crank Herbert.

Journey to the West: Conquering the Demons — *Demons* cede.

The Single Moms Club — Divorced from reality.

Need for Speed — Tires.
Veronica Mars — *Mars* I pan.
Enemy — Its own worst.
Bad Words — *Eff* that.
Le Week-End — Speed dimanche.
The Art of the Steal — Heists and lows.
Patrick: Evil Awakens — *Patrick* stewpid.
Better Living Through Chemistry — Dopey.
Divergent — Other nonsense.
Anita — Hill of beans.
Blood Ties — Sang-fraud.
God's Not Dead — He's just sleeping through this.
The Missing Picture — *Missing* accomplished.
Nymphomaniac: Volume 1 — The erector set.
300: Rise of an Empire — Greece ball.

Aaron Paul tries to feed his *Need for Speed*.

Sullivan Stapleton & Eva Green meet cute in *300: Rise of an Empire*.

Ricky Gervais has Miss Piggy & Kermit for dinner in *Muppets Most Wanted*.

Muppets Most Wanted — Felt bad.
Cheap Thrills — Bargain abasement.
Blood Soaked — Red sucks.
Finding Vivian Maier — Schmuck and *Maier*.
Rob the Mob — Fleece bites.
A Birder's Guide To Everything — Tweet thins.
Miele — Honey don't.
It Felt Like Love — Peter fondle.
Sabotage — Arnold bomber.
The Raid 2 — Second-*Raid*.

....

Under the Skin — Schlub-dermal.
Monster High: Frights, Camera, Action! — *Monster* low.
Breathe In — The stale air.
Cesar Chavez — *Chavez* ravine.
Mistaken for Strangers — *Strangers* on a drain.
Boys of Abu Ghraib — Beat my guest.
Dom Hemingway — Down by Law.
Alan Partridge — Jerky Coogan.
Nymphomaniac: Volume 2 — Sloppy seconds.
In the Blood — Plasma suite.

Afflicted — Sick and tired.

Frankie & Alice — *Frankie*, I don't give a damn.

Draft Day — *Draft* dodgy.

Rio 2 — Brazilian wacks.

Oculus — Rid-*Oculus*.

The Railway Man — The ham depot.

Only Lovers Left Alive — Jim charm mush.

Noah — Noah's *Arghh!*

Russell Crowe is sinkin' in the rain in *Noah*.

Black Widow (Scarlett Johansson) is not amused by 'look, ma, no hands' gag in *Captain America: The Winter Soldier*.

Teddy (Zac Efron) fraternizes with the enemy by tagging Mac (Seth Rogen) in *Neighbors*.

Captain America: The Winter Soldier — Cap and clown.

Perfect Sisters — Sissy, space chick.

Unthinkable — Don't even think about it.

Joe — Blows.

Hateship Loveship — Sunkship.

Transcendence — Transcend dunce.

A Haunted House 2 — Hauntdog.

Bears — A grudge.

Fading Gigolo — Fraud escort.

Make Your Move — To the exit.

13 Sins — *Sins* and outs.

....

Neighbors — Frat bastards.

Trailer Park Boys: Don't Legalize It – – Cracked weed.

Authors Anonymous — No one wants a credit on this.

Tasting Menu — Appetizer coarse.

The Demon Within — Inner skankdom.

The Final Member — Last dicks effort.

The Other Woman — Cheat *shee-it*.

The Quiet Ones — I won't hear of it.

Bryan Cranston is breaking nad in *Godzilla*.

Godzilla — Kaijus box.

From the Rough — Iron maidens.

Brick Mansions — Blockblister.

Walking With the Enemy — Simply treadful.

Locke — And load.

For No Good Reason — Steadman walking.

The German Doctor — Herr brained.

The Amazing Spider-Man 2 — WebMT.

Walk of Shame — From the box office to your seat.

Belle — Lavs.

The Protector 2 — Thai wracked.

The Bachelor Weekend — Stag potty.

Ida — Nun-conformist.

Wolverine helps Magneto, Mystique & Professor X reconnect with their younger selves in *X-Men: Days of Future Past*.

X-Men: Days of Future Past — X past facto.

Bad Johnson — Ball baring.

Mr. Jones — Chuck *Jones*.

Water & Power — An exercise in utility.

The M Word — The menopause that refreshes.

Chef — Boyardick.

The Double — Dual to the death.

....

Palo Alto — Skeevy suburban.

Devil's Knot — *Knot* for nothing.

God's Pocket — It's empty.

Legends of Oz: Dorothy's Return — *Oz* dragging.

The Wedding Video — Erase relations.

Million Dollar Arm — Pitch and putz.

The Immigrant — Drudge deport.

Wolf Creek 2 — Lupe fiasco.

Chinese Puzzle — Riddle management.
Half of a Yellow Sun — Sol survivor.
A Short History of Decay — It rots.
Blended — Puree nonsense.
Tracks — Path illogical.
Words and Pictures — School of visual arse.
How to Train Your Dragon 2 — Play dead.

Daenerys Targaryen instructs Hiccup in *How to Train Your Dragon 2*.

The Love Punch — Right in the bollocks.

The Angriest Man in Brooklyn — He hates hipsters.

Maleficent — A sticky *Wicked*.

A Million Ways to Die in the West — One way to die at the box office.

Filth — Scum one like you.

Night Moves — *Eek-o* disaster.

We Are the Best! — Feigned praise.

The Grand Seduction — Come-on now!

Jersey Boys — Piques and Valli.

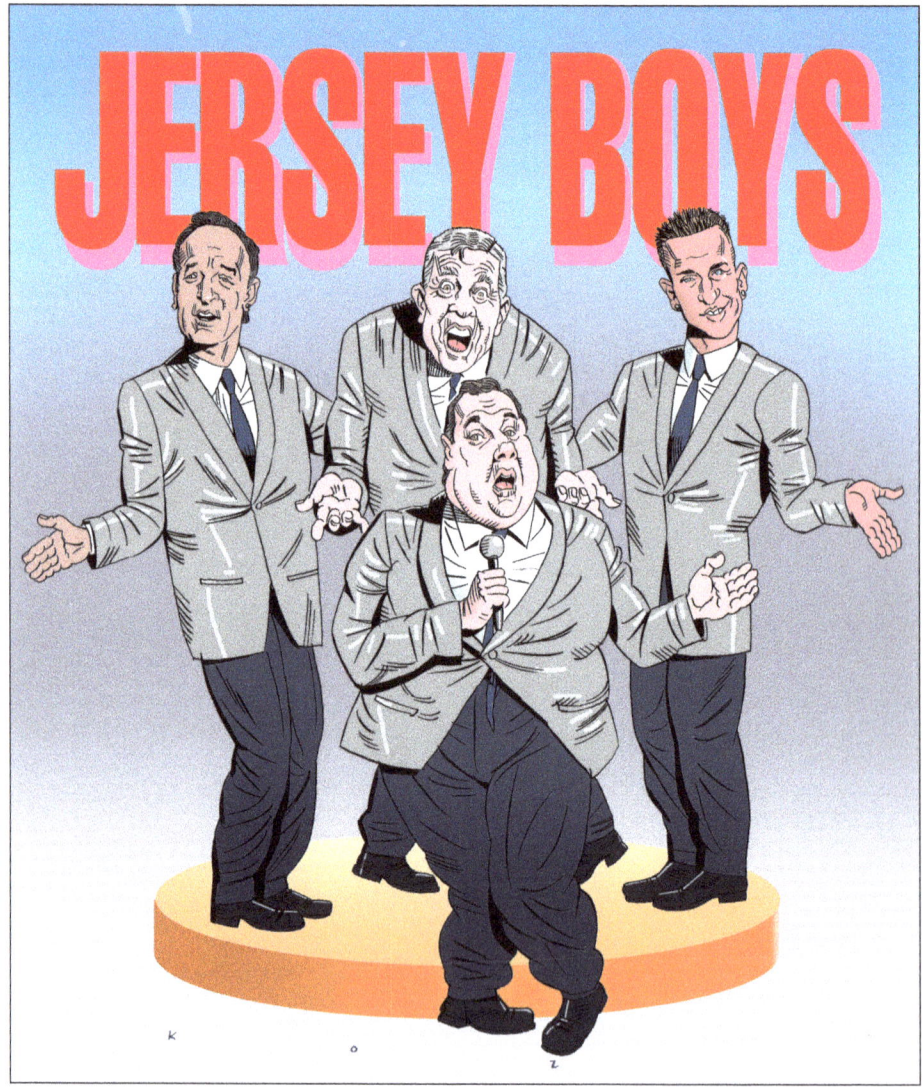

Bruce, Jerry & the Situation back up Chrissie in *Jersey Boys*.

Transformers: Age of Extinction — Roboglop.

Emoticon ;) — :-(

Edge of Tomorrow — Repeat after *meh*.

The Fault in Our Stars — Lunk cancer.

Obvious Child — Obvious everything.

Willow Creek — Pussy *Willow*.

Trust Me — To disappoint.

Supermensch: The Legend of Shep Gordon — Sinking *Shep*.

Citizen Koch — *Koch* zero.

The Case Against 8 — Prop hate.

22 Jump Street — *Jump* the snark.

Witching and Bitching — Boner hex.

The Rover — Roll over.

The Signal — Busy.

Violette — Stinking *Violette*.

Think Like a Man Too — Brain farce.

Venus in Furs — Mockee de Sade.

Robby sounds the alarm as a Decepticon attacks in *Transformers: Age of Extinction*.

....

Third Person — Not singular.

A Summer's Tale — *Été*-otic.

Exhibition — Flashing blight.

Tammy — Slob sister.

Earth to Echo — Repetitive stress syndrome.

Deliver Us from Evil — And this.

Premature — Too soon.

School Dance — Semen mixer.

The protagonists hear, see and speak evil, but are still adorably curious in *Dawn of the Planet of the Apes*.

Dawn of the Planet of the Apes — Monkey seize monkey doo.
America — U.S. noose.
Life Itself — Ebert's beast.
Wrinkles — Gray panters.
Me and You — Us weakly.
Beyond the Edge — Mountain douche.
Marius — Bar belle.
Boyhood — *Qué*-12?
Rage — Angers away.

....

A Long Way Down — But they reached bottom.
Road to Paloma — *Paloma* pick asshole.
Land Ho! — She works cruises, too.
Made in America — Jay-Zzzzzz.
Affluenza — Buggy rich.
The Perfect Wave — Curls on film.
Sex Tape — Premature ejectulation.
Planes: Fire And Rescue — Just fire.
The Purge: Anarchy — Flushed with pride.

Wish I Was Here — Braff pit.
Video Games: The Movie — Joyless shtick.
Fanny — Pack.
Mood Indigo — *Indigo* go.
I Origins — I phony.
Persecuted — Justifiably so.
Hercules — God awful.
And So It Goes — Peevish and butthead.
Magic in the Moonlight — Prestiregurgitation.
Lucy — Loo.
A Most Wanted Man — Dustbin Hoffman.
The Fluffy Movie — *Fluffy* nutter.
Happy Christmas — Seasonal invective disorder.
Very Good Girls — Angels and demeans.
Guardians of the Galaxy — Guardian-variety.

Gamora, Drax & Peter Quill prepare for battle as Rocket Raccoon, stationed in Groot's knothole, jumps the gun in *Guardians of the Galaxy*.

Leonardo, Michelangelo, Raphael & Donatello have a new boss in *Teenage Mutant Ninja Turtles*.

Bill Hader & Kristen Wiig play kookily suicidal siblings in *The Skeleton Twins*.

Teenage Mutant Ninja Turtles — Shell-schlock.
14 Blades — All dull.
The Kill Team — Soldiers of misfortune.
Into the Storm — Tempest in a pee pot.
Step Up: All In — Goosed steps.
The Hundred-Foot Journey — To *le WC*.
What If — We just stay home?
About Alex — *Alex* smack.
James Cameron's Deepsea Challenge 3D — *Voyage to the Bottom of the Ego.*
The Green Prince — Doubting Hamas.
After — Birth.

....

The Skeleton Twins — Have a bone to pick.
The Dog — Dog *duh* afternoon.
The Expendables 3 — Old war whores.
The Giver — Of headaches.
Frank — Head case.
The Trip to Italy — They tour it up.
Let's Be Cops — From badge to worse.
Life After Beth — *Beth* bye.
If I Stay — You go, girl.
When the Game Stands Tall — Streak hustle.
Are You Here — Unfortunately.

Mickey Rourke, Bruce Willis & Joseph Gordon-Levitt are ready to pull the trigger over femme fatale Eva Green in *Sin City: A Dame to Kill For.*

Sin City: A Dame to Kill For — Doxy moronic.

Love Is Strange — Humpy old men.

The One I Love — The two I hate.

The Prince — Of the shitty.

To Be Takei — George tacky.

Metro Manila — Luzon it.

Kink — Leer.

....

The November Man — Spy kids.

Starred Up — Starred/stop.

As Above/So Below — *Sooo* below.

The Congress — Lame-duck session.

Life of Crime — Potty larceny.

The Calling — A lower *Calling.*

The Last of Robin Hood — Err, ol' Flynn.

Teens, trapped like you-know-whats, hightail it in *The Maze Runner*.

The Maze Runner — A *Maze* in disgrace.

Jamie Marks Is Dead — Zippo *Marks*.

The Strange Color of Your Body's Tears — Weeping wallow.

Cantinflas — Ho-ho-hombre.

The Damned — If I do.

The Longest Week — Doze were the days.

Innocence — Pure nonsense.

The Identical — Twin bads.

Thunder and the House of Magic — Has the clap.

God Help the Girl — And the audience.

Trailer Park Boys: Don't Legalize It — Hitch cocks.

Wetlands — Drips and drab.

Smiling Through the Apocalypse: Esquire in the 60s — Mag and cheese.

Last Days in Vietnam — Mess Saigon.

Memphis — Tenn. commandments.

No Good Deed — Goes unnoticed.

The Drop — Of the jaw.

Atlas Shrugged: Who Is John Galt? — I shrug, too.

The Disappearance of Eleanor Rigby — Ah, look at all the lonely patrons.

Dolphin Tale 2 — Lacks porpoise.

My Old Lady — Tenant's match.

Duran Duran: Unstaged — An endurandurance test.

....

Gone Girl — Bye curious.

Born to Fly — Wings it.

Honeymoon — Married with chill dread.

Tusk — I slam the walrus.

I Am Eleven — And I diwected this movie.

Finding Fanny — Just reach behind you.

Bird People — Twitter feat.

The Guest — Overstays welcome.

This Is Where I Leave You — Abandon all dopes.

A Walk Among the Tombstones — Grave misgivings.

The Culture High — Blunt trauma.

Nick Dunne (Ben Affleck) looks high and low for missing wife Amy (Rosamund Pike) in *Gone Girl*.

Denzell Washington sweetens the deal in *The Equalizer*.

Cooper (Matthew McConaughey) encounters a superior lifeform that gives him a sign in *Interstellar*.

The Equalizer
— On an even kill.

At the Devil's Door
— Use the Beelzebuzzer.

The Zero Theorem
— Less than *Zero*.

Hector and the Search for Happiness
— Look elsewhere.

The Boxtrolls
— Troll la-la land.

The Two Faces of January
— I wanted to slap both.

Jimi: All Is By My Side
— *Jimi* crap corn.

Two Night Stand
— You'll sleep over.

Good People
— Does bad things.

Plastic — Credit snore.

....

Interstellar — Starbust.

Lilting — Southeast Gaysian.

Pump — Runs dry.

Small Time — Microscopic.

Men, Women & Children
— Everyone hates it.

The Judge — Downey softener.

Left Behind — No, the head's still up there.

The Good Lie
— Fib tickler.

Last Hijack — Jacked off.

The Liberator
— Bolívar watch.

For Those In Peril
— *Peril* jam.

Riggan (Michael Keaton) is torn between his former alter egos in *Birdman*.

Birdman or (the Unexpected Virtue of Ignorance) — Avian fluke.

Harmontown — Dan *ugghler*.

Nas — *Drovia!*

Annabelle — Leak.

Dracula Untold — Gore text.

Alexander and the Terrible, Horrible, No Good, Very Bad Day — All of the above.

St. Vincent — Murray pariah.

....

Whiplash — Humdrums.

Addicted — Left hooked.

The List — Less.

Automata — *Whatsamatta?*

One Chance — And they blew it.

Haunted State: Whispers from History — My murmur done told me.

Kill the Messenger — If he delivered this script.

Dead Snow 2: Red vs. Dead — Broken blizzard.

Kite — Drifty.

Meet the Mormons — Converts' sneakers.

Katniss salutes a new generation of rebels in *The Hunger Games: Mockingjay - Part I.*

The Hunger Games: Mockingjay - Part 1 — Pan 'em.
The Diappearance of Eleanor Rigby: Her/Him — She/It.
The Pact II — Fanny *Pact.*
Horrible Bosses 2 — Employ*eeks!*
Felony — Charge topper.
The Book of Life — *Dia de los Mierdas.*
The Best of Me — Is on the cutting room floor.
The Tale of Princess Kaguya — Ghibli jabber.
Dear White People — Honky dory.
Housebound — Shut-in impact.
A Girl Walks Home Alone at Night — Fall of the Persian vampire.
Listen Up Philip — Phil in the blank.
Diplomacy — Blaster of Paris.
Young Ones — Should avert their eyes.

Dumb and Dumber To
— *Dumb* star diving.

The Town That Dreaded Sundown — Scarry scarry night.

John Wick
— *Wick*, he leaks.

Ouija — Board to death.

Laggies — Fools behind.

White Bird in a Blizzard
— I just don't see it.

Force Majeure
— Farce mineur.

Citizen Four — The Abominable Snowden.

Stonehearst Asylum
— Lunatic cringe.

Nightcrawler
— News junky.

Goodbye to Language —
Waiting for Godard…to shut up.

....

The Imitation Game
— Genius *bah!*

Horns —
Evils and butthead.

Before I Go to Sleep
— At 10 minute mark.

Saw — Sadly, I did.

ABCs of Death 2
— Basic draining.

Big Hero 6 — *6* flags.

The Theory of Everything
— Hawking and talking.

Elsa & Fred
— Senior rom.

Happy Valley
— Pig Penn.

Fury — Tanks.

Jim Carrey & Jeff Daniels are still trying to cath in with gross-out humor in *Dumb and Dumber To*.

Alan Turing (Benedict Cumberbatch) encounters new technology in *The Imitation Game*.

Reese Witherspoon roughs it as Cheryl Strayed in *Wild*.

Wild — Bitch hiker.
The Penguins of Madagascar — Never takes off.
Women Who Flirt — With disaster.
The Babadook — Baba*dookie*.
Still Alice — Unfortunately.
Life Partners — Lady pards.
Exodus; Gods and Kings — Go down, Moses.
Inherent Vice — Pynchon putz.
Top Five — Shit list.
The Captive — Chained reaction.

Miss Julie — Suicide packed.
Jingle Bell Rocks — Sleigh me now.
Free the Nipple — Titters.
After the Fall — Like a bad trip.
Annie — Lummox.
Night at the Museum: Secret of the Tomb — Crypt creeper.
Mr. Turner — Paint expressions.
Goodbye to All That — Adieu date.
If You Don't, I Will — Don't you dare.

....

Big Eyes — Preachy Keane.
Winter Sleep — Wake me in April.
Into the Woods — Grimmshots.
The Interview — Kim junk *ewin'!*
Unbroken — POW woe.
American Sniper — Turkey shoots.
The Gambler — Ooze and odds.
Two Days, One Night — Weakened update.
Selma — King done come.

A Most Violent Year — Annumosity.

Ode to My Father — *Ode*: da pain!

The Woman in Black 2: Angel of Death — Inky shuffle.

The Search for General Tso — Tso-tso.

Magician: The Astonishing Life and Death of Orson Welles — Welles-hidden.

The Color of Time — Secs offender.

Dying of the Light — And the laughter.

....

V/H/S:Viral — Badder max.

By the Gun — Barrel of laughs.

Murder of a Cat — Shot puss.

The Foxy Merkins — Hairpiece virus.

Antarctica: A Year on Ice — Memories of tundra development.

Comet — Modesty blaze.

La Bête — Not a safe *Bête*.

The Hobbit: The Battle of the Five Armies — Tolkein resistance.

After their final appearance in *The Hobbit: The Battle of the Five Armies*, Bilbo & his friends return to the Shire to reclaim their old jobs.

Classic Critic's Corner

The Wolfman, Dracula, the Bride & the Monster are served a Halloween Frankenfood Feast by Vincent Price.

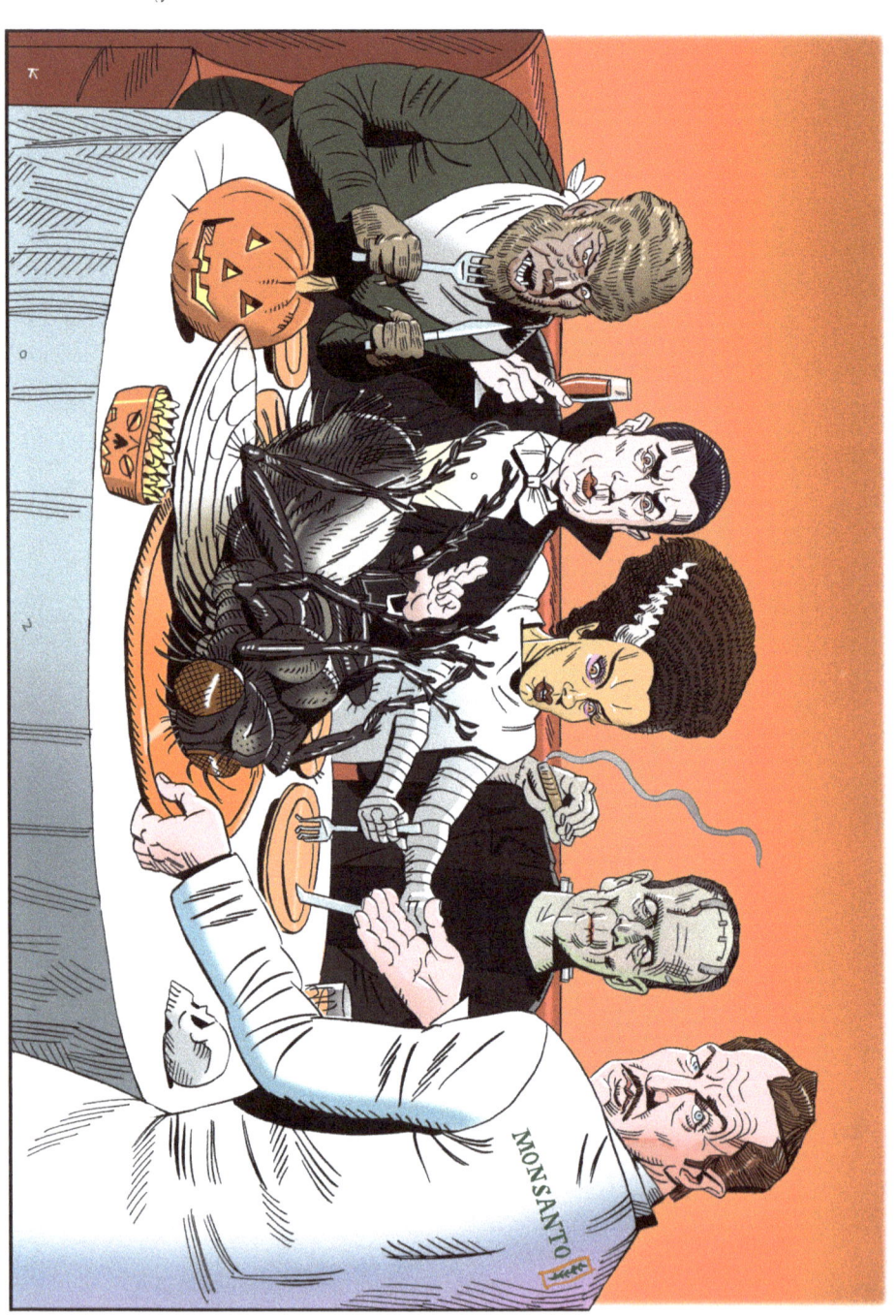

Monster of None

Each October in anticipation of my favorite holiday, Halloween, I fire up my Goldstar VCR and replay some of my favorite fear flicks. Josef always growls along with Chaney, Jr. These are classics from the 30s & 40s produced in Hollyweird, Karloffifornia as my frenemy, *Famous Monsters of Filmland's* Forry Ackerman, used to quip. Friend because he invited my fan mail, enemy because he never answered. Talk about a monster. *Grrr*. Oh, I just sounded like Chaney Jr. about to pounce on his papa. *Grrr*, Josef, *Grrr*.

Dracula (1931) — High blood pleasure.

Dracula's Daughter (1936) — The princess bite.

House of Dracula (1945) — It's undead construction.

Frankenstein (1931) — Sewing beast.

Bride of Frankenstein (1935) — Monster match.

Son of Frankenstein (1939) — Ygormaniac.

Ghost of Frankenstein (1942) — *Ghost* writher.

Frankenstein Meets the Wolfman (1943) — On JDate.

House of Frankenstein (1944) — Lab corpse.

The Wolfman (1941) — Chases his own tale.

The Werewolf of London (1935) — Moon ripper.

She-Wolf of London (1946) — Kind of a bitch.

The Invisible Man (1933) — Utterly transparent.

The Invisible Man Returns (1940) — Nobody notices.

The Invisible Woman (1940) — Not much of a looker.

Invisible Agent (1942) — Just try to get him on the phone.

The Invisible Man's Revenge (1944) — Wedgies.

The Mummy (1932) — Nile biter.

The Mummy's Hand (1940) — Of human bandage.

The Mummy's Tomb (1942) — Crypt off.

The Mummy's Ghost (1944) — Gangsta wrapper.

The Mummy's Curse (1944) — 'A remake with Brendan Fraser.'

Phantom of the Opera (1943) — Mess o' soprano.

Dr. Jekyll and Mr. Hyde (1931) — Schiz of death.

White Zombie (1932) — No-no shuffle.

Island of Lost Souls (1932) — Moreau less.

The Black Cat (1934) — A Poe excuse.

The Raven (1935) — Nevermore? You promise?

Mark of the Vampire (1935) — He signs in blood.

Mad Love (1935) — Maybe the first dozen issues.

2015

Boyhood's Ellar Coltrane, led by Patricia Arquette eyes role models David Oyelowo in *Selma*, Michael Keaton in *Birdman*, JK Simmons in *Whiplash*, Bradley Cooper in *American Sniper*, Baymax in *Big Hero 6*, Steve Carell in *Foxcatcher*, Benedict Cumberbatch in *The Imitation Game*, Eddie Redmayne in *The Theory of Everything* & Ralph Fiennes in *The Grand Budapest Hotel*. *Birdman* won Best Picture

Folks (Rasheed, at least) ask me if it isn't hard being a professional critic in an age when everyone and their Cousin Vinny has a blog chock full of 'reviews.' An opinion is like gas — hard to hold in, but foul if not yours.

These pretenders lack the true critic's one essential gift — an eye and an ear. A finely-tuned instrument honed by experience. E-Berts, as I call the untutored cyber scorners, have never seen a film made before the Aughts. Their 'classic cinema' is the first *Resident Evil* — Jason Reitman their Orson Welles.

Shut up until you've seen *All About Eve* on the big screen, YouTube boobs! Tho in my review I did summarize that one as '*Eve* ho.' Hypocrite much?

Loitering With Intent — That's the ticket.

Spare Parts — Robot's rules of order.

Blackhat — Hacks of violence.

The Wedding Ringer — Dead *Ringer*.

....

Paddington
— Poo bear.

Little Accidents
— On the carpet.

Match — Barre brawl.

Vice — Wicked bad.

Still Life
— Just sits there.

Human Capital
— Punishment.

Red Army
— Rinks off the hook.

Predestination
— Free VOD.

Let's Kill Ward's Wife
— With Ward cleaver.

Beloved Sisters
— Myth of sissy fuss.

Valley of Saints
— Vale of tears.

Mr. Brown (Hugh Bonneville) treats sugary-sweet *Paddington*.

Liam Neeson prepares for one more mission after *Taken 3*.

Vincent (Hugh Jackman) gets a pick-me-up from *Chappie*.

Taken 3 — Particular set of kills.

The World Made Straight — By Marcus Bachmann.

Preservation — In moth balls.

Something, Anything — Nothing.

The Boy Next Door — Neighborhood botch.

Black Sea — Sub zero.

The Humbling — Humiliating.

Cake — Punt *Cake*.

Manny — Petty.

....

Chappie — AI-AI-*Ohhh!*

Son of a Gun — Small bore.

The Duke of Burgundy — Ron's cousin.

Black or White — Race to the bottom.

The Loft — *Loft* at sea.

Project Almanac — Project dumb way.

Wild Card — What the deuce?

Timbuktu — Mali-ficent.

Girlhood — Gang bangers.

Johnny Depp's *Mortdecai* meets his mindless match.

Mortdecai — Mortdefai.
Back Street Boys: Show 'Em What You're Made of — Styrofoam.
Suburban Gothic — 'Burb buried suits.
Alien Outpost — Or Outhouse?
Seventh Son — *Seventh* heavin'.
The SpongeBob Movie: Sponge Out of Water — All dried up.
Jupiter Ascending — Ass sending.
Lovesick — Veni, VD, vici.
Enter the Dangerous Mind — Brain of terror.
Boy Meets Girl — Trannie sez.
We'll Never Have Paris — Need I say amour?
Kingsman: The Secret Service — The life of spy.
The Rewrite — Draft dodger.
Girl House — Sluttites.

Smith & Robbie keep their eyes on the prize in *Focus*.

Focus — Dash scam.
Nailed — You need like a hole in the head.
What We Do in the Shadows — Dumb and umbra.
Gett: The Trial of Viviane Ansalem — *Gett* outta here.
Hot Tub Time Machine 2 — Stupor soaker.
The DUFF — Get off it.
McFarland USA — Crass country runners.
Queen and Country — Service dog.
Digging Up the Marrow — Bone dry.
The Second Best Exotic Marigold Hotel — Jaipuractivity.

Unfinished Business — Not quite ready to flush.
These Final Hours — Ticked off.
Maps to the Stars — Tourtuous.
The Salvation — Saved by the bull.
All the Wilderness — Where the wild things err.
The Lazarus Effect — Razing the dead.
'71 — Not worth the Troubles.
Everly — *Hubba hubba* Hayak.

....

Wild Canaries — Cheepers creepers.
Kidnapping Mr. Heineken — Beer haul.
Run All Night — On the toilet.
It Follows — Sh_ _.
Home Sweet Hell — Heiglian logic.
Cymbeline — Symbol lean.
Champs — Glove triangle.
The Wrecking Crew — Hell-razers.

Eva — Brawny.

Seymour: An Introduction — I'd like to see less.

Muck — True grime.

Insurgent — Uprise and fall.

Accidental Love — A screw-up.

Danny Collins — Fraught *Collins*.

Spring — Break.

Do You Believe — Cred alert.

Kumiko, the Treasure Hunter — Bury the lead.

Tracers — Not of logic.

Fifty Shades of Grey — Semi-hard cheese.

Jamie Dornan & Dakota Johnson submit a moviegoer to *Fifty Shades of Grey*.

Serious shoeaholic *Cinderella* (Lily James) dumps the Prince (Richard Madden) for *The Cobbler* (Adam Sandler).

Cinderella — EllaOL.

The Cobbler — Heel thyself.

Sean Penn hunts down his old nemesis for revenge in *The Gunman*.

The Gunman — Cross Penn.

Amour Fou — *Fou* fighters.

Jauja — Not on my mind.

Can't Stand Losing You — Police bust.

Home — Run!

While We're Young — Nihil *Young*

Serena — Serenal failure.

....

The Riot Club — Amok raker.

Last Knights — Joust for the hell of it.

Welcome to New York — Straus con.

The Kidnapping of Michel Houllebecq — Ain't no Houellebecq, girl.

My Italian Secret: The Forgotten Heroes — Goombah, yah. My lord!

Furious 7 — Car and drivel.

Woman in Gold — Klimt biscuit.

Kevin James has a cow in *Paul Blart: Mall Cop 2*.

Every Day — Routine.
The Squeeze — Golf coarse.
The Heart Specialist — Cardiyuks arrest.
Beyond the Reach — Shite of the hunter.
The Longest Ride — Caca-and-bull story.
Ex Machina — A bot for sin.
Kill Me Three Times — Thrice 'im.

....

Clouds of Sils Maria — Swiss mess.
Black Souls — Wet mob.
Freetown — Missionary impossible.
Desert Dancer — Iran pall.
Lost River — Ebon flow.
Dior and I — Christian mingle.
Broken Horses — Saddle snores.
The Sisterhood of Night — Shudder stock.

Paul Blart: Mall Cop 2 — Tub of Blart.
The Culling — For the cullible.
To Write Love on Her Arms — Tats all she wrote.
Ned Rifle — Half-cocked.
5 to 7 — Odds you'll like this.
Seeds of Time — Pips squeak.
Cut Bank — Wuss Fargo.
The Dickumentary — Dick doc.
W.M.D. — Mess destruction.
Boychoir — Vocal fries.
Electric Slide — In the low 80s.
That Guy Dick Miller — Miller low life.
Season of the Witch — Snored and sorcery.
The Time That Remains — As I stare at my wristwatch.
The Green Hornet — Buzzworthless.
The Dilemma — De lemon.

Kevin Hart tries to make Will Ferrell more gangsta with corn rows in *Get Hard*.

Get Hard — Soft poor corn.
True Story — Just lies there.

Unfriended — Face booked.

Child 44 — Russia to judgment.

Monkey Kingdom — Happy scampers.

Monsters: Dark Continent — War and beast.

Tangerines — Keen peel.

The Age of Adaline — Sour *Adaline*.

Little Boy — Lost.

Adult Beginners — False start.

Blackbird — Rah-rah aves.

Kung Fu Jungle — Kicking and scheming.

The Forger — Like a three-dollar bill.

Avengers: Age of Ultron — Marvel slab.

Avengers Thor (Chris Hemsworth), Black Widow (Scarlett Johansson) & Captain America (Chris Evans) assemble to celebrate *Age of Ultron*.

The Water Diviner
— Dowses off.

Just Before I Go
— I undo my fly.

After the Ball
— We smoke.

14 Days — Too week.

Brotherly Love
— Philly fanatic.

Far From the Madding Crowd — Hardy har har.

Welcome to Me
— Ego-terrorism.

Hyena — Laughing ass.

Ride — Stuff.

Iris — Merde doc.

Days of Grace
— Notional futbol league.

Cas & Dylan
— Who *Cas*?

Far From Men
— And perfect.

Soul Boys of the Western World —
Spandau Ballet slipper.

Comedy Dynamics Presents: Bill Hicks — *Hicks* nix dix pix.

Hot Pursuit — Trailer trash.

Maggie — Maggoty.

Playing It Cool – Over the chill.

The 100-Year-Old Man Who Climbed Out the Window and Disappeared
— A goner.

Saint Laurent — Yves of destruction.

I Am Big Bird — Big, yellow, taxing.

The D Train — Reunion square.

Skin Trade — Dullph Lundgren.

5 Flights Up — Vacant stairs.

The Seven Five — Police scammer.

Pitch Perfect 2 — Ick capella.

Russell Crowe taps a gusher in *The Water Diviner*.

Maniacal Immortan Joe, speeding along with Nux (Nicholas Hoult) & Furiosa (Charlize Theron), reveals his true identity to Max (Tom Hardy) in *Mad Max: Fury Road*.

Mad Max: Fury Road — Diesel zapper.

Good Kill — Drones town massacre.

Slow West — *Whoa* is me.

I'll See You in My Dreams — After I nod off watching this.

Every Secret Thing — The young and the ruthless.

Time Lapse — *Lapse* a luxury.

Where Hope Grows — Moss.

Two Shots Fired — Blanks pace.

The Connection — The fringe *Connection*.

Animals — Fur cryin' out loud.

Dark Star: HR Giger's World — Giger counter.

Our Man in Teheran — Iran weasley.

The Film Critic — Plots and pans.

Tomorrowland — Predictable.

Chris Pratt & Indominus Rex are too drowsy to roar in dinosnore epic *Jurassic World*.

Jurassic World — Train Rex.

Poltergeist — Just ghost to show.

When Marnie Was Here — Anime of the people.

Chocolate City — Brown peeper packages.

Aloft — Overhead wrack.

The Human Centipede II — Seg*mental*.

San Andreas — Faulty.

Aloha — Hello? *Goodbye!*

Survivor — Keeps on ticking…me off.

Barely Lethal — Tiny danger.

Walking on Sunshine — Junkbox musical.

Heaven Knows What — This is.

Results — Gym jones.

Gemma Bovary — Gust of Flaubert.

Spy — Cherry spy.

Entourage — Past its dude date.

Love & Mercy — Wilson flips.

Testament of Youth — Lost will and *Testament*.

Insidious: Chapter 3 — Psychic squealer.

A Pigeon Sat on a Branch Reflecting on Existence — Then shat on this.

Hungry Hearts — Cardio fatness.

Charlie's Country — Australian, back out.

The Nightmare — A snooze.

Electric Boogaloo: The Wild, Untold Story of Cannon Films — Schlocksmiths.

Freedom — Fries.

Inside Out — Emotional wreck.

Joy, Fear, Disgust & Sadness welcome the new embodiment of Anger in *Inside Out*.

toas**ted 2**

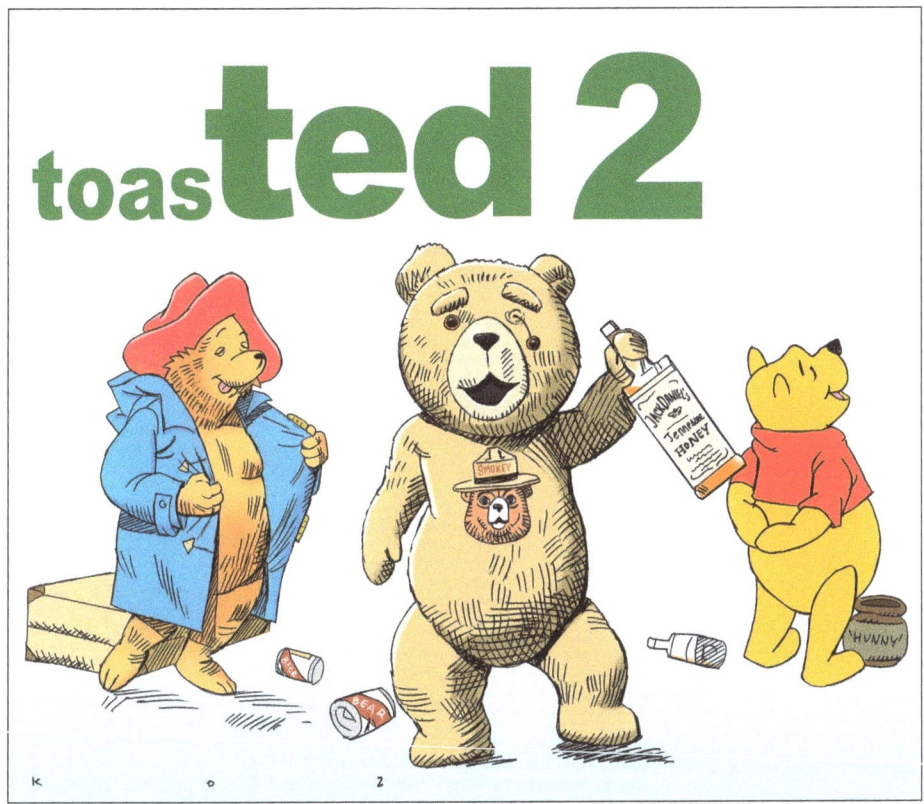

A tatted Ted proves a bad influence on his bear bros in *Ted 2*.

Ted 2 — Stuffed and nonsense.
Madame Bovary — Suicide squeeze.
Me & Earl & the Dying Girl — Buss terminal.
The Wolfpack — Out of the lupe.
The Tribe — The tripe.
Set Fire to the Stars — And throw the director on the pile.
The Yes Men Are Revolting — The whole cast is.

....

Live From New York! — Forlorn Michaels.
Debug — Up de ass.
Dope — Yeah, you, buying the ticket.
Infinitely Polar Bear — *Polar Bear* plunges.
The Overnight — Prime cot.
Manglehorn — Ill Pacino.
Eden — *Eden* rot.
The Face of an Angel — Amanda knocks.

The adorable pischers are back, scaring up a quorum of ten for worship services in *Minions*.

Minions — A barrel of flunkies.

Burying the Ex — Ex compost mentis.

United Passions — FIFA and dumb corps.

Max — Dog star.

Big Game — Hunt's catch-up.

Tap World — Toe jams.

Escobar: Paradise Lost — Narco-leptic.

....

A Little Chaos — Nobody *Chaos*.

Batkid Begins — To cloy.

The Little Death — *Le petit mort*ification.

Magic Mike XXL — Strip stakes.

Terminator Genisys — Mech and cheese.

Faith of Our Fathers — Nam commital.

Cartel Land — Narc *nyuk nyuk*.

Amy — Whinehouse.

Jimmy's Hall — Irish missed.

Robot Overlords — The last wound up.

Zarafa — Giraffe dodgers.

Self/less — More of *less*.

The Gallows — Hang it all!

What We Did on Our Holiday — Jaunt disease.

Boulevard — A thorough fair.

Nowitzki: The Perfect Shot — Dork Nowitzki.

Trainwreck — Starring aimless humor.

Mr. Holmes — Old Holmes weak.

Irrational Man — Woody? Afraid so.

The Stanford Prison Experiment — Lab brats.

Joe Dirt 2: Beautiful Loser — Soiled.

Caffeinated — Joe dirt.

Ant-Man — A damn ant.

Famous Nathan — Frank.

Do I Sound Gay — Lisp price.

The Look of Silence —*Shh*ut-eye.

Pixels — Game men's health crisis.

Southpaw — Staggering.

Paper Towns — Teen and sympathy.

Unexpected — Belly whopper.

Smosh: The Movie — *Smosh* pit.

The Chosen — Not by me.

Five Star — Gang blank.

The Young Kieslowski — Pole dunce.

Ant-Man, Marvel's tiniest hero, spars with one of its biggest.

Mr. Fantastic uses his super powers to retrieve the Human Torch's keys from The Thing as Invisible Girl looks on in *Fantastic Four*.

Fantastic Four — Four on the floor.
Phoenix — Ash hole.
Vacation — Ditz takes a holiday.
The End of the Tour — *Tour* bust.
Listen to Me Marlon — Brando X.
A LEGO Brickumentary — Thick as a brick.
Extinction — So over.
Best of Enemies — Vidal statistics.
That Sugar Film — Empty calories.
Northmen: A Viking Saga — Fjord alert.
I Am Chris Farley — Chris folly.
Jenny's Wedding — Jenny from the *blecch*.

The Kindergarten Teacher — On the tyke.
The Gift — Left by Spot.
Ricki and the Flash — *Ricki*-tick.
The Diary of a Teenage Girl — 16 scandals.
Dragon Ball Z: Resurrection 'F' — *'F'* dat.
Shaun the Sheep — Should be shorn.
Dark Places — Yeah, turn off the projector.

....

Call Me Lucky — I missed this.
Cop Car — Screen siren.
Kahlil Gibran's The Prophet — And loss.
Straight Outta Compton — Film *NWA*.
She's Funny That Way — No *Way*.
Mistress America — Regretter Gerwig.
Return to Sender — Immediately!
People Places Things — Dad frank act.

Tom Cruise performs a death-defying stunt in *Mission: Impossible – Rogue Nation*

Mission: Impossible - Rogue Nation — Wrecking Cruise.

Tom at the Farm — *Tom* thump.

Enchanted Kingdom 3D — The crawl of Nature.

Meru — Climb disease.

Exeter — Grad slam.

Fort Tilden — Artificial hip.

Walt Before Mickey — Cel theory.

Amnesiac — Mnemonic plague.

Air — Ball.

Final Girl — Lass hurrah.

American Ultra — *Shit* or *Get Off the Pot*.

Hitman: Agent 47 — Special offer.

Sinister 2 — *2* silly.

After Words — Librarian of congress.

Grandma — Dozes.

The Man From U.N.C.L.E. — Cry, *U.N.C.L.E.*

Napoleon Solo & Ilya Kuryakin take out their double agents in *The Man From U.N.C.L.E.*

No Escape — Craptrap.

Digging for Fire — Exhuming beings.

Learning to Drive — Reverse psychology.

Some Kind of Beautiful — *Beautiful* reamer.

Being Evel — The *Evel* dead.

The Curse of Downers Grove — Hex fiends.

Mateo — Mariachi banned.

Slow Learners — Rom calm.

Blood Cells — Irony poor.

The Lost Key — Locks and a schmear.

We Are Your Friends — Who needs enemies?

A Walk In the Woods — Stupid human treks.

Owen Wilson tries to act his way out of a paper bag in *No Escape*.

....

The Visit — Pop Pop fizzle fizzle.

Quay — *Pasa?*

Station to Station — Trainspotty.

Memories of the Sword — Mind shaft.

War Room — Medium prayer.

The Perfect Guy — Too good to beat u.

Goodnight Mommy — Mom genes.

Time Out of Mind — Director, too.

Coming Home — Greet is good.

Pop Pop & Nana welcome an unwanted guest in *The Visit*.

Whitey Bulger (Johnny Depp) shows a small-time hood how to really deflate a ball in *Black Mass*.

Mark Watney (Matt Damon) is stranded, abandoned and utterly alone on the Red Planet in *The Martian*.

Black Mass — Whitey fraud.

A Brilliant Young Mind — Take a brain check.

Sleeping With Other People — In the same theater.

90 Minutes in Heaven — Plus another 31 in Hell.

Breathe — Artificial respiration.

12 Rounds 3: Lockdown — Give it arrest.

Welcome to Leith — Whiteness protection program.

Captive — Lemme outta here.

....

The Martian — Maroon jive.

Maze Runner: The Scorch Trials — Burnt dumber.

Sicario — A la cartel.

(T)ERROR — (T) minus.

Everest — Nepal slip.

The Captive — Order in the caught.

Cooties — Scabies, it's you!

Peace Officer — Police staid.

Gotti: Three Generations — Heir guns.

Steve Jobs (Michael Fassbender) offers an unsuspecting consumer a poison Apple.

Steve Jobs — *Jobs* search.
Pawn Sacrifice — Chess record.
Being Canadian — Drear, *eh?*
The Intern — Aide is enough.
Hotel Transylvania 2 — Tomb service.
The Green Inferno — Cannibalshit.
99 Homes — Eviction no dice.
Ashby — Ass be.
Finders Keepers — *Keepers* weepers.

....

Drunk Stoned Brilliant Dead — Lampoon tang.
Roger Waters The Wall — By peeing on it.
The Walk — Petit farce.
Freeheld — Ail and farewell.
Labyrinth of Lies — Come what mass.
He Named Me Malala — Heroine chic.
Partisan — Communal bash.
Shanghai — China dull.
Addicted to Fresno — Off the hooked.

Richie Lanz (Bill Murray) unveils his latest Afghani singing sensation in *Rock the Kasbah*.

Rock the Kasbah — Pashtun project.
This Is Happening — Sad to say.
A Christmas Horror Story — Jack Frost ripping at your nose.
Stonewall — *Que-er* No. 1!
Pan — The Peter Principle.
Knock Knock — No one's there.

....

Big Stone Gap — In the plot.
Victoria — Falls.
Trash — Know thyself.
The Final Girls — Last-bitch effort.
Prime Ministers: Soldiers and Peacemakers — Begin, the Rabin.
Goosebumps — Freakin' Stine.

Macbeth — Dread Scot.

Crimson Peak — Piker's *Peak*.

Room — *Bah!*

Beasts of No Nation — Kiddie hawk.

Woodlawn — Hail Mary. Pass.

Meadowland — Grassy null.

Truth — Rather. *Not!*

Experimenter — Trial in error.

Paranormal Activity: The Ghost Dimension — Haunt toad.

The Night Before — Eve ardent.

A Ballerina's Tale — Off pointe.

Bastard — Who's your Daddy?

....

Bridge of Spies — Classified sad.

All Things Must Pass — Like a kidney stone.

The Last Witch Hunter — Spell check.

Suffragette — Voter fraud.

Jem and the Holograms — Semi-precious *Jem*.

I Smile Back — Low beam.

Nasty Baby — Nasty, baby.

Bone Tomahawk — Chop screwy.

Attack on Titan Part 2 — *Titan* ick.

India's Daughter — Indian rapee.

In *Macbeth*, Michael Fassbender plays yet another ruthless, power-mad tyrant.

Tom Hanks negotiates with his opposite number in the Cold War thriller *Bridge of Spies*.

Extraordinary Tales — Poe diddley.

Heart of a Dog — Brains, too.

Burnt — Sooey chef.

Scouts Guide to the Zombie Apocalypse — Scout willies.

Our Brand is Crisis — All politics is loco.

The Wonders — Bee geez.

Love — All that jizz.

Carter High — Somebody must've been.

Sex, Death and Bowling — Lane excuses.

Spectre — AutoBond.

Bond (Daniel Craig) faces off with cat-lover 'Oberhauser' (Christoph Waltz) in *Spectre*.

Creed — Rocky blah blower.

The Price We Pay — That's the ticket.

Freaks of Nature — On freek?

Hard Labor — Well, it wasn't *easy* watching this.

The Peanuts Movie — Brown nos.

Spotlight — Fathers goose.

Brooklyn — Ex-paddy.

Trumbo — Shrimp.

Miss You Already — Gal pales.

The Hallow — *Hallow* threat.

A leathery Rocky (Sylvester Stallone) helps young fighter Adonis (Michael B. Jordan) train in *Creed*.

Jackson Heights — Queens of the damned.

Love the Coopers — Christmas hams.

The 33 — And a turd.

By the Sea — Jolie pity.

Shelter — Streets weeper.

Heist — Heavy lifting.

Very Semi-Serious — *Gag!* cartoons.

Legend — The latest Krays.

....

Secret in Their Eyes — Blink and you won't miss it.

I Am Thor — God of blunder.

Mustang — Wild Turkey.

Criminal Activities — Pity larceny.

The Good Dinosaur — Dino mite.

Victor Frankenstein — Loser *Frankenstein*.

The Danish Girl — Danish twist.

Janis: Little Girl Blue — Joplin, misery.

Killing Them Safely — Tased and confused.

Katniss (Jennifer Lawrence) finally gets the chance to hunt down the evil President of the future in *The Hunger Games: Mockingjay - Part 2*.

The Hunger Games: Mockingjay - Part 2 — Mocking J-Law.

The Lady in the Van — Dirty harridan.

Youth — Anasia.

Chi-Raq — Chi-ite.

A Royal Night Out — Princess cruises.

Krampus — *Claus*trophobic.

Hitchcock/Truffaut — Bored of directors.

....

Life — Dean wormer.

In the Heart of the Sea — Whaleboner.

The Big Short — At a loss.

Body — Shaming.

Don Verdean — Bent *Verdean*.

The Girl in the Book — Cover one's ass.

Boy and the World — Down *Boy*.

Sisters — Relative sleaze.

Star Wars: Episode VII - The Force Awakens — *Force* square.

Alvin and the Chipmunks: The Road Chip — Cow Chip.

Son of Saul — Saul for naught.

Carol — Alt.

He Never Died — Mouth-breather.

The Emperor's New Clothes — Threads bare.

Where to Invade Next — Moore of the same.

Point Break — Surf's no purpose.

Joy — Miracle mope.

Anomalisa — Puppety love.

Other People's Children — Kid vicious.

....

The Revenant — Off the beaten trek.

The Hateful Eight — Octogoners.

45 Years — Union specific.

Concussion — Head games.

Daddy's Home — Father blows best.

The Genital Warriors — F Troop.

Close Range — Fire at swill.

River of Fundament — Fun demented.

The Messenger — Kill *The Messenger*.

SPOILER ALERT! In *Star Wars: Episode VII – The Force Awakens*, Luke Skywalker undergoes gender reassignment surgery and, as Leilu, woos and marries Han Solo. The couple then adopts reformed Stormtrooper Finn.

Leonardo DiCaprio of *The Revenant* & Kurt Russell of *The Hateful Eight* meet on the brutally frozen frontier and try to out-grizzle one another.

2016

It's survival of the A-List as Matt Damon in *The Martian*, Charlize Theron in *Mad Max: Fury Road*, Anger in *Inside Out*, Christian Bale in *The Big Short*, Eddie Redmayne in *The Danish Girl*, Sylvester Stallone in *Creed*, Leonardo DiCaprio in *The Revenant* & Saoirse Ronan in *Brooklyn* all vie for the Oscar held by the Grizzly (*not Black*) Bear. *Spotlight* won Best Picture (*www.*).

I write this while still fuming over M*ad Max: Fury Road* (starring Tom *ever so* Hardy) losing Best Pic to *Spotlight,* which dropped the 'bombshell' that Catholic priests in Boston abused their flock. Look, I'm from the big city (near Muncie) and we all knew what went on 'backstage' at St. Ignatius' and no, when Father Tom said 'Take, eat', you would never. I'm not saying priests shouldn't be defrocked, but so should Heidi Klum — did you see what she wore on the Red Carpet? And note to Chris Rock: I never felt so white or so guilty. And I loved it!

Here is a final smattering of pans for films released just before we went to press.

Lamb — Kabomb.

Sherlock: The Abominable Bride — *Er,* shlock.

Diablo — Hell no!

....

The Forest
— *Forest* tuckers.

The Masked Saint
— Rassle dazzle.

Anesthesia
— Put out.

Trust Fund
— Put away.

Cherry Tree
— Leaf off.

The Abandoned
— Leave it alone.

The Treasure
— Razz bury.

Sweaty Betty
— *Betty* boob.

Anger of the Dead
— S'tiffs.

Eisenstein In Guanajuato —
Mex Marx the spot.

Natalie Dormer approached by a woodland creature in *The Forest.*

Dirty Grandpa Dick (Robert De Niro) lasciviously lathers up Lenore (Aubrey Plaza) as dirty ol' pals Woody & Roman leer on.

Dirty Grandpa — Old blue *oys*.

Ride Along 2 — Doomed patrol.

13 Hours: The Secret Soldiers of Benghazi — Bent, gassy.

Norm of the North — Polar ass cap.

The Benefactor — Give back.

400 Days — Space doubt.

A Perfect Day — Like death warred over.

....

Band of Robbers — *Robbers* barren.

Moonwalkers — Craters.

Intruders — Break in bad.

In the Shadow of Women — Elles stinko.

Detective Chinatown — Angry Thai raid.

The 5th Wave — *Wave* bye-bye.

The Boy — I kid, you not.

Ip Man 3 — *Ip* pain.
Mojave — Just deserts.
Synchronicity — Jibe turkey.
Terminus — At wit's end.
Exposed — Flash slob.
Monster Hunt — Brute awakening.
Prescription Thugs — Dirt pharma.

....

Monkey Up — Ape is enough.
Martyrs — Sacrificial hams.
Eternity: The Movie — Endless shrimp.
The Finest Hours — Not these 2.
Jane Got a Gun — Jane *d'oh!*
Fifty Shades of Black — Massachistic.
Kung Fu Panda 3 — Pander bare.

Mei Mei gets a whiff of Po in *Kung Fu Panda 3*.

Baird Whitlock (George Clooney) need ask 'Et tu, Coene?' as the cinematic siblings stick it to him in *Hail Caesar!*

Hail, Caesar! — *Caesar* squalid.
Everybody's Fine — OKStupid.
El Clan — *Clan* of corn.
Greater — Shoulda been.
Lazer Team — Laze. Err.
Mountain Men — Hill of beings.

....

Rabin, the Last Day — *Yitzhak*ademic.
Portrait of a Serial Monogamist — Faithfully snores.
Pride and Prejudice and Zombies — Austen shitty limits.
The Choice — Opt out.
Rams — *Rams* stuff.
Dad's Army — Military rank.
Regression — Low-yield return.

Southbound — Dicks o' inferno.

The Club — Fathers and sins.

Misconduct — Dr. sues.

Tumbledown — Unsound of music.

All Roads Lead to Rome — Via not amused

The Pack — Dog *ciao*.

A Melody to Remember — Hum dingier.

How to Be Single — Dated.

Deadpool — Dead poo.

Zoolander 2 — Pose and cons.

Metaparodies *Deadpool* & *Zoolander 2* collide as
the Merc with the Mouth is unmasked as the Jerk with the Pout.

Clavius (Joseph Fiennes) can't figure out the Nazarene's levitation trick in *Risen*.

Risen — Easter bummy.
Glassland — Irish weep stakes.
Remember — To forget.
A War — Martial matters.
Touched With Fire — Dud poets' society.
Already Tomorrow in Hong Kong — Slow bloat to China.
Bad Hurt — Wise achers.
The Witch — Spells disaster.
Race — Dark meet.
Embrace of the Serpent — Uncoiled for.
Forsaken — Lone deranger.
The Great Gilly Hopkins — Brat worst.

Rolling Papers — Keeps a spliff upper lip.
Busco Novio Para Mi Mujer — Kissy faze.
We Are Twisted F•••ing Sister! — Grade D Snider.
Snowtime! — Flakes out.
Gods of Egypt — Horus' ass.

....

Triple 9 — A heisty retreat.
Eddie the Eagle — Ski doo.
Crouching Tiger, Hidden Dragon: Sword of Destiny — Kicks and giggles.
Only Yesterday — Takahata airbag.
Tricked — See gulls.
Backtrack — Retread.
A Country Called Home — Texas toast.

Tina Fey in a *Whisky Tango Foxtrot* scene set in Afghanistan as the Taliban AD prepares to cry 'Cut!'

Whiskey Tango Foxtrot — Kabuldygook.

The Last Man on the Moon — Apollo creed.

King Georges — Gorge us, Georges.

London Has Fallen — Collapse in judgment.

Zootopia — Animal crappers.

Knight of Cups — Tarotdiddle.

Desierto — Arid. Roll on.

The Other Side of the Door — Knob hell.

Cemetery of Splendor — Boneyard animals.

They Will Have to Kill Us First — High on Mali.

Road Games — Shoulder pain.

The Brothers Grimsby — The elephant 'n' the womb.
10 Cloverfield Lane — Cellar dweller.
The Lobster — Will do in a pinch.
The Young Messiah — Goo Goo God God.
The Divergent Series: Allegiant — *Allegiant* airs disease.
The Program — Lance end.
The Bronze — Medalhead.

....

Midnight Special — On the runt.
Krisha — Hairy *Krisha*.
My Big Fat Greek Wedding 2 — Fetid cheese.
I Saw the Light — Angst Williams.
Get a Job — Fool employment.
Born to Be Blue — Chet braker.
Batman v Superman: Dawn of Justice — From Bat to versus.

The Dark Knight (Ben Affleck) challenges the Man of Steel (Henry Cavill) on an even playing field in *Batman v Superman: Dawn of Justice*.

www.ingramcontent.com/pod-product-compliance
Lightning Source LLC
LaVergne TN
LVHW070013090426
835508LV00048B/3384